VELVET

VELVET

POEMS

William Fargason

Curbstone Books / Northwestern University Press
Evanston, Illinois

Curbstone Books
Northwestern University Press
www.nupress.northwestern.edu

Printed in the United States of America

10 9 8 7 6 5 4 3 2 1

Library of Congress Cataloging-in-Publication Data

Names: Fargason, William, 1988– author.
Title: Velvet : poems / William Fargason.
Description: Evanston : Curbstone Books/Northwestern University Press, 2024.
Identifiers: LCCN 2023051462 | ISBN 9780810147232 (paperback) | ISBN
    9780810147249 (ebook)
Subjects: LCGFT: Poetry.
Classification: LCC PS3606.A684 V45 2024 | DDC 811.6—dc23/eng/20231101
LC record available at https://lccn.loc.gov/2023051462

*For my father
who chooses
not to read*

the person
passed into the flame, becomes the flame—

—William Carlos Williams, *Paterson*, Book III

CONTENTS

I

HOUSE MADE OF GUNS

In the house made of guns in the city
made of guns on the street lit with lead,

my father sits building a new room.
This is to be my room, with a scope

for a window, the crosshairs
of white wood across the glass

framing the yard with the hollowed-out
pine tree crooked from the last storm.

I watch him as I always did as a child,
through a crack in the door. He is good

with his hands, could take apart
any machine you gave him

and learn how to put it back together
in breaking it down. He sands the wood

of my doorframe, which will hold
a door I will hide behind years later.

My father's tongue is the trigger
of the gun in the house made of guns.

My mother and my sister and I
wait for the primer to be dimpled

by the firing pin like a thumbprint
left in the sand. The whole house is

cocked and waiting for the first shot
of the morning. My father is smiling,

or maybe wincing, deep in his work.
I walk the golden floor made

of bullet casings. What happens
when you live in violence so long

that it's what you call home? This house
must fall. I will flip the safety off

every gun. I will aim each barrel into
another. I won't kneel in the shadows

when he says kneel. I will taste
gunpowder on my tongue.

APOLOGY

My father would take the washcloth
and wring it out with both of his hands,
the water falling like rain from a heaven
he controlled. He would wash my back,
and I would watch him teach me

tenderness—the way he would gut
a deer, holding the ribs like a dance partner
as it swayed from the skinning shed
on a rope. The soap left a thin film
on the water like a cloudy mirror. I could feel

his cruelty, as if each bath was nothing
more than his prayer of forgiveness
to the son he had hours earlier hit
with a belt like he was driving a nail
into a wall, a period into a sentence.

There was a largeness inside him
I watched grow small, a father becoming
a failed man or an afternoon bent
on sunset. After my bath he would sit
on the edge of my bed and always

apologize, which never felt genuine
since it kept happening, the apology never
for his temper or who he was,
but for getting soap in my small eyes,
right before they closed on sleep.

THAT SUMMER AT SEASIDE

we slept in the attic   in two twin beds
and I was off my meds   by choice
this time   I thought it would be a good idea
it had been   months without a panic attack

I was   doing well enough   I was
wrong   the roof of that beach house
leaked in the night   waking me   to the sound
of rain inside the room   you stayed
asleep   I laid out towels to catch
the storm   pooling on the buckled hardwood
it must've leaked before   the maple boards
turned gray as ash   I could see
even in the night   I could not fall back asleep

I needed to be next to you   in the morning
your family downstairs   didn't understand
why I was acting strange   I thought I was
doing well enough   still ashamed
to tell them   I was medicated
or not   that those were withdrawal effects
or worse   simply how I felt   unbalanced

the sand rose   like a storm surge
I could see   from the window overlooking
the street   laid with bricks   small channels
full of rain drying in the sun   I could not go
with your family to the beach   their cooler
full of cans of shandy   inside I stayed
for hours   the hum of my body
down from the medicine   sobering up
my brain chemistry   I thought
I would see more clearly   without

you   came inside   asked me to join you
I headed upstairs to get my things
the damp towels   crumpled across
the floor   a field of sleeping newborns

PUNCH LIST, 1994

My father takes my hands and places them
on each joystick of the Bobcat. I'm too small

to reach the pedals, so his feet tip up the bucket
full of jobsite debris in the air above me.

I watch broken Sheetrock hit two-by-fours
and crack apart like packed snow. It feels

triumphant to watch the scarred metal bucket
eclipse the high noon sun, the bucket's teeth

slowly coming into view like a giant sea creature
rising out of the water next to a boat I am on

in the middle of the ocean with my father.
He is teaching me control, *pull that lever*

right there back, good, now turn the Bobcat left,
the machine jolting like a roller coaster

as it mounts its first incline. He is teaching me
power, and in these moments I can almost

forget how much he scared me, even then,
holding me in his lap beneath the pulled-down

safety bar. With each tip of the bucket
he is teaching me how to be him, to claim

a birthright of dirt and Tyvek, of Skoal
and Leatherman blades that sharpened

framer's pencils behind the ears of men who speak
with the calluses on their hands like a clay tablet

of cuneiform in each handshake, of proving
something by what you've built or torn down.

GASOLINE

Father, our house is on fire
and I fear you lit the match.

You held it in your teeth
like my tiny body, like a fish

struggling to swim upstream.
But you were not always awful,

which made you more of a lock
I had to crack. I took two bobby pins

from the drawer of mom's dresser
when she wasn't looking.

I spent all night in front of
that lock. No luck. Some mornings

before school I'd awake to you
rubbing my back, and even then

I woke scared of your silence
in the dull light. I know the cause

of the fire, this is not a mystery
any longer, but I am walking

through each burnt room.
To find where it started,

I only have to find the room
with the most damage.

A SILVERFISH IN THE CHILDHOOD

picture of my father   pressed in the glass
my father's year-old face   soft focus

and bodiless   his teeth coming in   I tap the glass
the silverfish's small body   doesn't move

doesn't fall   to the wood frame   as I'd expect
looks more like a tiny lobster   than an insect

who survives   between books on a shelf
its dead body   a temporary monument

in the museum of my family   on the wall
of what was my sister's bedroom   the silverfish

an insect who eats paper to live   no history is safe
from this centimeter of gray dust   that sought out

this picture as its meal   that only thought of
a way in   but not a way out   in the edge

of the photo   the year 1959   the silverfish
tried to consume   that year   corner by corner

reverse the past   or at least   its representation
my father's young brain   forming each fold

learning from his father   which family member
was okay to hit   my father's childhood

a broken branch   he would break   into smaller pieces
over his knee   if only that silverfish

could've eaten those days   before they happened
stopped my inheritance   if only it could've

spared me   wrath   a smiling baby who'd grow up
to throw in a fit   whatever was closest

at children   who'd grow up   to rub my back
during the sermon   who'd search for the knot

the old-testament God   and the new-testament God
are the same God   the same package deal

if only that silverfish   could've made it across
the picture   across the soft hair   on my father's brow

I had a chance   not to be here   standing in front
of this picture   I could've not been here   that erasure

wanting its help   wanting to fade
from the frame   I could've not been here

I could've been paper passed through a body

OPEN HOUSE

as a child   I went with my father
to his open house   a house he had just built
a house in the Parade of Homes   the street

lined with pennant flags   from the mailbox
to the brand-new maple   the flags moved

like leaves in the wind   I followed behind
my father   quiet through each room
my step matching his   my small feet

making imprints in the roll of plastic rolled out
on the floor   like a red-carpet premiere

and he showed me   the kitchen   furnished
with fake fruit and fake plants   as if someone
already lived there   and sometimes when he was

busy talking to a nice rich couple   I'd sneak
off into the other rooms   up the stairs

or down a hallway   I'd think this room
could be my room   my bed could go
there   my books there   the carpet held

no memory of his anger   his voice echoing
like a dropped glass   against the vaulted ceiling

and in that room   my room   I would feel safe
away from him   in the emptiness   thinking
he built this   thinking he built this for me

ANKYLOSING SPONDYLITIS AS CONDUCTOR AND BRAKEMAN

anxious about sleep   I can't
my bed not   a grave   nor a raft
nor any melodrama   I make of it
but the turning of   my body
in the night   my spine inflamed

by my arthritis   my immune system
my own body attacking itself   like a cartoon
conductor   on a cartoon train
pulling every red lever   all the way down
until it breaks off   the needles

on the gauges   spinning around
like my ceiling fan   the glass
of each gauge   cracking into
jagged lines   like nerves up my spine
reminding me I'm awake   should be

trying to sleep   the sheets untucked
and flying past me   like ghosts
trying to keep up   with the speed
as the steam paints the cartoon sky
gray   and begins to fill my bedroom

a chronic pain   never gets better
only lesser   only choosing when
to come back   choosing when
to switch   the railroad track
as I approach   in the distance

TRACING THE PAIN

it's hard to explain how tired I feel   each day
my autoimmune disease attacking my bones
at the hip joint and spine   I limp down the hall

to the water fountain where I joke but am serious
about needing a cane   at my old job
there was one guy who brought a cane

to work each day   but not out of need
more of an accessory   when asked about it
he said something about using it to beat the ground

in front of him to check for snakes in Georgia
where he was from   which sounded like
horseshit to me   and a good way to get bit

I think it won't be long before my father
needs a cane   every year I watch my father
from whom I inherited my eyes and work ethic

and this disease   grow stiffer as he walks
from bedroom to kitchen   blinking a lot
and asking what's for breakfast   we have so little

in common   it has almost become a joke
on car rides alone trying to fill
the silence   he didn't know he had it

until I found out   tracing the pain
through waiting room after waiting room
until I learned the word   for what we shared

SONNET WITH CHRONIC ILLNESS

Lord each day   there is a flame in my hips
in my back   I can't even walk outside
without pills   Lord why would you
give me this disease   build my bones

like a wrought-iron fence I can't cross
Lord each day   I barely make it
outside to the mailbox   only to find
letters full of dust Lord   still no reply

Lord when the one body you gave me
attacks itself   who do I blame
Lord do I get another   one day
with you   if so   how will I know

myself without this body   how will I
recognize myself   without this pain

RIVER

Lord I trust you   I trust
myself not to trust you
when the snow laces the power line

the window   and even my hand
against the glass doesn't melt it

my heart is so far from the river
I swam in as a kid   its crawfish
we would find under the rocks

the chill on our skin   of the cold water
Lord I felt your presence   there

in the banked mud against
my feet   were you there with me
Lord   I used to speak to you

in the dark of my bedroom
you are the father who never

comes home from work   I want
to say I love your voice even though
I can't hear it   I have forgotten

how to pray except during panic
Lord I don't want only to feel

close to you when I think I'm dying
I want a river covered in
snow   I want a knock on the door

ODE TO KLONOPIN

O first responder   O pinprick
of smoke   weld my synapses
like two sponges   becoming one
every shadow   filling with light
O blanket of reality   I enter a field
where you are gatekeeper   a field

it seems   everyone else walks through
daily   O patched hole in my tire
O little chemical pearl   O break in case
of emergency   O bowling bumpers
I come to you   needing only you
I trace my wrists my neck   my pulse
unfindable   O warmth of my mother
O June   sometimes I split you

on the scored line   take half
I know   I will be back for more
the anxiety always   electricity
a thunder in my body   O surge

protector   keep me safe for the night
for four to six hours   let me sleep
without waking mid-attack   again
keep me   until I can't keep you anymore

PEOPLE AS SEASONS AS PEOPLE

Over time, two objects of different weight
      —stalagmites or snowfall—will hit the ground

at exactly the same time, every time. She is
      getting dressed, pulling her bra straps over

her shoulders, she pulls one, and then
      the other. It's morning. She washes her face

in the bathroom sink, and from the bed,
      it sounds like a gutter filling with rain.

I pull a clean shirt out of my suitcase,
      walk into the kitchen. On the table, a jam jar

and toast. Once the jar has been opened,
      it must be refrigerated, she says as I sit down.

Over time, even a soft wind can knock
      down a spiderweb. She is not a fixed variable,

as I am. She slices a grapefruit down
      the center, then hands me my half

on one of her grandmother's plates.
      Over time, these things break. With a spoon,

she digs into each section of the soft pulp.

AIM

Over and over I shot into a bank of red clay
a hundred yards down a strip of bush-hogged
pasture. My father paced behind me with a sock
full of sand, said *Here, set it on this.* I smiled at the puffs
of dust that rose and dissipated.

                    Eventually, there were
targets: paper plates at first, X's he'd drawn
in permanent marker, then empty soda cans he filled
with water, hung with fishing line from branches.
Once hit, water sprayed out, the cans blossoming
into metal flowers.

                  What I thought was harmless
wasn't. I held the gun in my hand, shifted it
to the other: the swirled grain of the oak stock,
the sling's cracked leather, my reflection a warped
blue shadow on the steel barrel.

                    Then came phone books
that didn't move. Opened up, the holes on the cover
were cigarette burns but sliced through the pages
in waves, ripped up whole neighborhoods
of last names, half of the alphabet busted into
yellow confetti: *Goodbye Peterson, Richards, Ryan.*
Goodbye Baker, Bennett, Berkman, Brighton. Goodbye.
Inside, real bullets mushroomed no larger than olives.
Goodbye Anderson. Goodbye Derricks. Goodbye, goodbye.

ARS POETICA

I kept my mouth
closed for many years.
I listened to the wind
play the dark branches

like a cello. The rain
in the street had gathered
into a pool I could see
myself in. My hands

left my pockets and joined the air
as if receiving an offering
from a priest in the dirt. I kept
my mouth closed

for many years, and then,
I opened it.

VOX

Voice is a nail I kick out of the road. Voice is
        busted glass roughly in the shape of my head,
                is every unknown number I never called
        back. Voice is a child letting go of a balloon,
my father coming home after a long day of work,
        still ignoring me at the table. It's two birds
                crashing into each other. All the trees
        the birds won't land in. Voice is every beautiful
woman who made me lose track. It's losing
        my voice from screaming, then blaming it
                on allergies again. Voice is eating my hands
        one finger at a time, and it's blue, always blue.
A button my hands are too cold to fasten.
        Or a board game with no pieces. Voice is ash
                on the tongue, coal in the lungs. Voice is
        my brother at the bottom of a well. Voice
is eating dessert first, always, as much as it is
        repeatedly drawing a blade across a sharpening
                stone. Voice is every sock I've ever lost. It's
        the eight layers of paint on the hutch my grandmother
gave me. Voice is walking barefoot but holding
        my shoes. It's a simple machine, a pulley
                or a lever, it's a hungry kiln, a panorama
        of doors I stand outside of. Voice is holding
your hand for the first time. Voice is skipping
        a stone across water, counting the skips it makes
                before sinking. Voice is standing on a shore
        I can't see any other shores from. Voice is riding
coach even though I paid for first class. Voice
        is waves of heat off asphalt, and it's a problem
                I don't want to solve, either. Voice is both grass
        covered in frost and my mother's hand
on my forehead. Voice is a seed in the throat, a flower
        in the hand. Voice is a wooded dark I walk into.

WHEN MY FATHER TELLS ME TO MOVE ON ALREADY

I keep looking out the window   see the rotting fruit
each offering to God   the flies circling the altar
specks of dust in the eye   my father pulls both arms

close to his chest   gets defensive   no one wants
to be told they're abusive   especially abusers
no one wants to be   the bad guy   the window frames

my body   standing in the living room   my father
in his easy chair   my mother   a footnote
in his abuse   this conversation   she rides shotgun

in the getaway car   sits silent as always   letting him
do what he wants   the man is head of the house
her God told her   can you blame someone

for following their God   up the wrong trail
on the mountain   burned fields below   the view
she lets him do the talking   at least she listens

instead of asking for more first fruits   only to watch it
from afar   as it turns back into seeds   in the sun

ARROWHEAD

The deer chews a tuft of grass
but never swallows, and moves through

the night like fog. I stand on the edge
of the field unable to move closer

or farther away. I look down
and my feet have become two pines

rooted in place. The deer rises
into the air, suspended—

its hooves four black diamonds.
My father named this field

Arrowhead after the chiseled quartz
he found in the dirt, this field

on his property line. As a child
I watched him kill this deer, then after,

smear its blood on my face—
a fingerful down my nose, across

my forehead. It felt like sweat
I couldn't wipe away. On the other side

of the clear-cut, smoke rises, the small field
center-lit with droplets of dew.

Fire starts on the tree line, frames
the deer, backlit beneath the moon.

The fire burns but never spreads,
hovering like a knife of sunrise

behind the trees. I can't see
my father, but I know the shot

will be fired, the cocked rifle always
against his shoulder. I want to yell

at the deer to run but my mouth
is full of leaves. The deer finally drops

from the air. Roots of bone grow
from its head, then fall to the ground

with no sound. The antlers plant
themselves in the wet earth and glow

underground like veins of lightning.
When the deer shakes its coat,

ash falls and hangs in the air
longer than it should like a dirty halo.

The fire smells clean like rain.

II

ARK

When I decided to build the ark I knew
I didn't deserve to be on it. Ark

of my doubt, built of cypress and pitch,
of every clean and unclean beast—

not just two by two but seven
by seven. Ark of my sins twenty feet

underwater, of rain, of so much rain,
of a small fire under a covered awning

on the bow of the boat. I wanted to take
that one long piece of pine out of the fire

and torch the whole, burn the top half
until the water underneath put it out,

knowing I could never fully burn anything
floating on water just like I could never run

from God without Him seeing me crouched
behind a thicket in the edge of the woods.

Ark of my labor in a pile of kindling,
a pile of straw among the horseshit

and lambs. I talk to them, as if they understand.
I walk the edges and look down

at every patch of land now covered
in wrath. I look down in the water and see

my own face. Ark of my wife, of my sons,
of my sons' wives, of every child they held

in their bodies, turning in them, lost
in the flood of their becoming,

of that small child not knowing
what they will inherit on this new earth,

not knowing what will grow or die
in this new life. I understood why God

would want to destroy everything He created—
the distant gray of the mountains,

the green of each tree. But just killing
something doesn't make it go away. Ark

of the mind, of my hands I built
in faith, O Lord, of weeks without sun,

of the old world, let me start
over again, let me start again.

ELEGY WITH STEAM

When I was sick with a head cold, my head
full of pressure, my father would soak a washcloth
in hot water, then ball it up, wring it out. He would
open it above my head, then place it against

my face like a second skin, the light around me
disappearing entirely except through the spaces
between the stitching. I would inhale the steam
in that darkness, hearing his voice on the other side,

otherwise almost devoid of any other bodily sense
but the warmth and depth of his voice, as if
I had already died and was on the other side
of life waiting for the sickness to lift, but I wasn't.

I was still on this earth, the washcloth going cold
on my face, my body still sick, and my father still
there when I opened my eyes, as he always was,
there to give me warmth before going cold again.

ELEGY WITH MY
GREAT-GRANDMOTHER'S PIANO

On weeknights when she would play,
my great-grandfather would search
the house for where he hid
his whiskey bottles—floating in the toilet

tank or lying face up in his daughter's
old saxophone case like a tiny coffin.
Once, his daughter found a bottle
in a pile of twisted blankets in the attic

like a mummified body or a newborn.
And she left it there. Downstairs, the sound
of Bach filled that old house, as he got more
and more drunk, the notes swelling

inside him. Some nights his son
would stand between them to keep
him from hitting her again, grinding
I hate you I hate you through his teeth

like a dirty prayer to a god who wouldn't
listen or who would pray the same back.
Despite the bruises, she played on,
the music she brought the only peace

that house would know. Not long after,
she and the kids sold all the guns
and knives in the house to a pawn shop
in Avondale, anything to take that possibility

out of the air, and when they came home
they found the piano on its side by the curb,
keys missing like a broken smile, its lid
splayed ajar like a cut-open belly,

each string and felt hammer curled
as splintered kindling—and one of its legs
was snapped off, as if he beat the noise
back out of it with its own wooden body.

LETTER

Erasure of a letter sent by my great-grandfather to President
Roosevelt about funding for the school board in the county where
he taught. His letter was reprinted by the Fannin County Times
on Thursday, August 1, 1940

I don't suppose this   will ever
get through

     I   understand   a man
             must throw around
himself   in the
   chance   it might. I am
                      this
Idea of yours   developed
through the difficult years
     As   always
       some of these ideas were
   good   some were not   I

might live more abundantly
           I know   I am
just a drop in this Great River
                 all along
I have flowed,
speeding up the Current, that we
might reach the Sea. I am

          the
     Problem
With   birth

troubled with   everything
                    Now here is our prob-
lem.   Power
              came into this
                                land. A
dam was built, the place flooded.
                        in this mountain
              only the valleys are
                        being flooded
not   farmed

    This
        all   matters

              I will have to run

                        this
            Life

                        Yes I
know   the goal
                is
you
                        must close. Yes
I will move on, but "What of them?

why

        Can't you help us?

    I remain,
    Worried

    I am

                    by
    the Wayside.   I am
            deadly serious.

FIRST PLEA

my sister's son   doesn't speak yet   he should
a year behind   half his age   I took off my shoes
at my parents' door   I was upstairs trying to   walk quietly
as to not wake him   his soft brown hair   messy in his crib

each bar like a line of a song   he can't sing yet   any loud
noise sets him off   crying again   all the things he's seen
in his own home   his father throwing his mother
into a shelf   each box of cereal   falling to the floor

with her body   he is learning   but for now   he's asleep
at my parents' house   the length of a divorce could feel
like a dream upon waking   last night I played him
a song on my guitar   let him pull on the strings   let him

let out anything   he almost broke them   I tried to
show him how to strum   tried to show him   there can be
a gentleness to the noise   later when I went to see if
he was up   he was talking in his sleep   full sentences

moving his hands   as one does when on the telephone
with someone very far away   and in their absence
one paces the room   phone in hand   as I got closer
I could hear him repeat   *mama why not   mama*

why not   mama why not   until I rested my hand
on his head   to wake him up   to bring him back
from wherever it was he was   he pulled his red blanket
tighter around his chest   and wouldn't wake

WATERLINE

as a child   my mother would make me
go back inside   to check
her curling iron   to see if it was still
on   I would trace   the cord   from handle
to prong   like I was reading a story
reading each line   over and then over again
to find the meaning   as a child

my mother   wouldn't let me
shower during   a thunderstorm
she said   a bolt could hit   the waterline
and it'd travel out   the showerhead
into my bones   like in *Tom and Jerry*
when Tom is struck   the blue
around his body flashing   his bones
off and on   and now as an adult   I check

the stove   three times before leaving
always in a pattern   so now I think of
my mother as I unplug my toaster   coffeepot
electric kettle   anything heat-producing
anything that could   catch fire must stay off
I check it three times   in sets of three
before I leave my apartment   or go to bed
I speak it aloud   until I'm convinced
that is off   that is off   that is   off

just like I learned years ago   a current
of electricity   a jolt of panic
through my arms   I now have medication
for that   a switch I try to turn off   even
though the breaker box   is waiting
the powerlines   in the distance
my mother's arms   above me

SONNET WITH BARE BRANCHES

Lord I don't   Lord after I go
I don't want to be remembered
as unkind   as unable to hold
the door for my neighbor Lord

when the fruits of the spirit
are the signs of you   how do I forgive
myself of myself   how Lord do I
when each season a new species

in my body goes extinct   Lord
how do I extend like a green leaf
fighting winter with its greenness
Lord how do I stay   kind toward

the sky   when the only voice I hear
is the one that echoes back

FLARE-UP

some days   on good days   I forget
each bone in my spine   is trying
to join   like a train fusing
into one long boxcar   on the tracks
I wake up   in pain   there is
no position I can lie   to not feel
that flame   the muscles sore
to the touch   around my spine
that terrible bone   that holds me
to this earth   like a flagpole
flying a flag of my disease   my illness
that won't lift   there are days
I forget the flag flies   there are
weeks the wind   doesn't blow
but I can't lower it   fold it   fly
a new flag   of my joy   of each step
I take out into the sun   so I stand
beneath the flag   below my pain
and put my hand   over my heart

FAMILY REUNION

The morning after the reunion my father and I
drove to the family grave plot outside a small town
in south Georgia, across a set of train tracks,
which looked smaller than they should've been,

as if the train that rode them was only one
built in the imagination. One headstone
displayed the family name, as if the entirety
of my lineage was bound to that tract of earth.

Next to it, my great- and great-great-grandparents,
uncles, aunts. Names I never knew, or names
I was named after. My father and I posed
for a picture, which, even at the time, felt wrong.

I didn't smile. No more than fifty feet across from
our plot was a Confederate soldier memorial
filled with smaller headstones, pointed at the top,
and a red and blue flag waving on its pole

in the hot August air. The limestone looked washed
in gray, and the plot was shaded by cedars
like our family's. My father didn't want to stop
and read the plaque with me, so I read by myself—

fifty-one soldiers were buried here, but among
the uncounted, one Black hospital attendant.
The headstone read *Unknown*—as if the only thing
remembered was their race and their job,

buried behind enemy lines. Every other headstone
had a tiny Confederate flag stuck in the dirt
in front of it—the kind a small child might wave
as a parade passes. But this unknown attendant,

who cared for the wounds of those fighting
to keep them enslaved, had an American flag
in front of their grayed headstone. I wanted to
kneel down, pay my respects to someone whose name

was erased by those who didn't take the time
to learn it before burying them. I wonder if they
stood in the morning light and looked out
at the sun rising through that hospital window

before pulling the stitching thread as fine
as a spiderweb deftly through the air, then wrapped
the wound like a present. And then onto
the next bed, the next man wincing against

the pillow as the attendant brought the ether
to the surgeon then held the man down
with four others as the man's leg was amputated
just above the knee. I wonder if the man

on that bed knew who was saving him. I wanted
to rip every red and blue X out of the ground,
but I didn't. My father calls this *history, just
what happened.* I knew my family, and one day

myself, would share the same earth, eaten
by the same worms and feeding the same trees
above. I knew that someone long before me
chose this plot across from this memorial,

that I could never dig each relative up and replant them
somewhere less shameful, the train tracks
would always go from one direction to another,
the cedars have already grown from what was buried.

on the wall   of my father's hunting cabin
above the kitchen table   hangs a picture

of my father   a pink boa around his neck
like one you'd buy   in the discount bin

at a party store   with one feathered end
flung over his shoulder   his hat stuffed

with Spanish moss   from the trees
in the background   to form a gray wig

his left arm is extended   his wrist limp
and fingers spread   his pose is meant

to mock his idea of   a gay man
this pose is how   he believed they posed

this picture is not only   framed
but also photoshopped together   to say

Hog Hunting Monthly   and below
the hot pink text   are fake articles

"Top 12 Ways to Serve Your Bacon"
and   "How to Squeal Like a Pig"

as if this picture   this cover   were on
a newsstand   before I went off to college

my father said   he punched his roommate
when he found out he was gay   and I'm not sure

why he told me this story   other than
to teach me a lesson   to pass on

his violence   like when he yelled at me
for forgetting the bullets   back at camp

he turned   the jacked-up camo golf cart
back around so hard   he almost threw me

into the dirt   and the entire hunt
he sat with me   still as a stone

and I was almost glad   I had the gun
just in case   and in the shooting house

he didn't joke   but later he would
my father somehow thought   this photo

on the wall was funny   he would laugh
about it   with his hunting buddies

as they sat around the table   the blood still
on their forearms   the deer hanging

by its legs   in the floodlight
of the skinning shed   my father passing me

the best cut of steak   then wiping his knife
against his napkin   I stood later

in the doorway   of that hunting club
and felt the softness   of his flannel

tossed on the couch   I followed his eyes
in the frame   to the gun rack on the wall

its wooden arms   cradled full
of hunting rifles   loaded and waiting

ELEGY WITH A HURRICANE

on the edge   of my parents' backyard
a deer feeder   spins out corn

down silver-fluted trays   that hovers
in the light   like a hurricane

seen on a satellite map   red-green
then green-red   my mother

watches the deer   each morning
when the feeder goes off   at seven

she stands at the window   alone
she says she can't believe   my father

would kill   such a peaceful creature
I don't say   I can

VELVET

1.

Once the season begins, it's rare to see a buck still in velvet. They shed it mid-March, the strands peeling back to reveal the bone beneath. Since veins went up through each tine to grow the antlers, the shedding of velvet is bloody. The bucks will scrape against a tree trunk to pull the velvet off, the velvet hanging like a shawl or tinsel from their heads.

2.

My father once killed a six-point still in velvet with his bow. Bow season starts in October, rifle season in November. My father killed it less for the size and more for the rarity. I know this because it's shoulder-mounted in his living room. The fur turns whiter every year due to the sunlight through the window it's next to.

3.

My father stands in the middle of the room, surrounded by elk, moose, and mountain goat heads. I see the dust on the fur of the deer closest to me. I trace the sunlight up to the window where the dust hangs in each beam of light like bits of kelp pulled outward by undertow. I feel the pull of that room each time I walk in, the audience of eyes.

4.

The term ["velvet"] originally arose from the fine hairs on the antler, but is now used specifically to indicate the antler's stage of growth: before it calcifies (ossifies). In nature, antlers will fall off after they have ossified; thus, collecting fallen antler doesn't provide the desired "velvet."

5.

Companies now sell capsules full of ground antler velvet. It's believed to help accelerate healing, especially in the joints and bones. Some believe it provides strength—what the deer leave behind we pick up to eat and heal. If the pills don't work, they make a liposomal spray.

6.

Quartered away, quartered toward. Broadside. I knew the best shot with each angle of the deer. How the heart is just off the curve of the shoulder. How if the bullet passes through the shoulder when quartered away, it will hit the heart, lungs, and then the gut. The exit wound always larger than the entry wound. A simple gut shot will mean tracking for hours. But if it's a lung shot, the blood on the ground will have tiny air bubbles in it. The blood trail was like a story to me when I was young. I wanted to read each page to find out what happened next.

7.

I got my first rifle at six years old—a .22 called a Chipmunk. This model was made for kids, no more than two-and-a-half feet long. I killed a squirrel with that gun when I was eight, held it by the tail while my father snapped a Polaroid, his bloody thumbprint on the white border. By ten, I'd killed a deer and joined something larger than myself, the history of death.

8.

Antler is a simple extension of bone, so it has a calcium-phosphate matrix of hydroxyapatite, $Ca_{10}(PO_4)_6(OH)_2$, integrated with smaller amounts of calcium carbonate ($CaCO_3$); its composition is similar to that of human bones.

9.

I inherited a chronic arthritis condition from my father called *ankylosing spondylitis*. If left untreated, my bones will fuse at the joints, starting in my hips and lower spine. *Ankylosing spondylitis is an autoimmune disease*—my body fighting itself—*and is a type of arthritis of the spine. It causes swelling between your vertebrae, which are the disks that make up your spine, and in the joints between your spine and pelvis. The disease is more common and more severe in men. . . . These problems often start in late adolescence or early adulthood.*

10.

Over time, pain and stiffness may progress to the upper spine and even into the rib cage and neck. Ultimately, the inflammation can cause the sacroiliac and vertebral bones to fuse or grow together.

11.

Consuming deer antler *may have some anti-inflammatory action, useful for arthritis.* It *benefits joints and ligaments.*

12.

The deer in Courbet's *Remise de chevreuils au ruisseau de Plaisir-Fontaine* (1866) are half shadows, gathered around a creek. The buck, quartered away, rubs his gray face against a tree. The doe next to him sits facing the edge of the water, the pale light like the quiet they hide in. My wife comes up behind me, notices I've been looking at this painting for a long time, asks if I want to head upstairs to the Impressionist exhibit. I stare back at a small buck, a spike, against the greens darkening, that edges one foot in the water.

13.

From the paper-stretched table where I sit, I watch my doctor's hand tracing the hip socket on the diagram as he shows me the first place my bones will fuse. Each morning at roughly the same time I take Celebrex. My bone disease cannot be reversed, healed, or cured. *The pills help lower inflammation,* my doctor says.

14.

On YouTube, I listen to a man explain the process of harvesting DAV, or Deer Antler Velvet. He recommends two to six capsules a day, taken with or without food.

15.

At the end of every season a deer sheds their antlers. If you find these sheds in the woods, you can save them for the rut, knock two of them together over and over to simulate two bucks fighting. The other bucks in the area will run to the noise. The sound is the sound of competition, of one male against another, a victor. The first shed I found this way was chewed all over by a squirrel, seeking calcium.

16.

It took four years to diagnose my bone disease. The doctors told me it was a stress fracture from playing soccer. My father always thought his pain was due to the physical nature of his job—lifting lumber and fifty-pound bundles of tar-backed roof shingles, or laying tilework in a bathroom on his knees.

17.

The stag's antlers are made of lead in the Nicolas Coustou sculpture *Chasseur terrassant un cerf* (1703–1706), or *Hunter Slaying a Stag*. They are the unintentional focal point against the white marble. They are broken off above the brow tine and first point, respectively. As I stand below the hooves of the creature, I realize the statue is almost life-size. This statue, *carved from a single block of marble*, used to sit *at the foot of the Rivière cascade* in *the park of the Château de Marly (near Paris)*. The hunter is in mid-strike, as if going in for the killing blow, but the stag's tongue is already hanging out of its mouth. The hunter is in mid-strike, but his sword is missing a blade.

18.

I sold my .30-06 to a local gun shop last year because I didn't use it anymore. My father knew this meant something. Above the man behind the counter were two rows of AR-15s, each one with a different clip, barrel, or stock.

19.

To harvest the antler velvet, the deer's antlers are removed while they are under local anesthesia. I imagine the dart laced with sedatives shot through a gun not unlike one I've used or owned.

20.

The cut antlers are bathed in boiling water and air dried, and then further dried in the shade or by low temperature baking.

21.

After I killed a doe at ten years old, I posed for pictures. I sat in the beams of the four-wheeler headlights and held the deer up by the ears—there was nothing else to hold it up by. I was too young to skin it myself, but my father took a fingerful of its blood and painted it under my eyes, down my nose, and across my forehead. Later, in the small shower of that hunting cabin, the blood turned pink and ran down my body toward the drain.

22.

The pills of deer antler velvet contain insulin-like growth factor (IGF) I and II. *IGF-1 is a powerful anabolic hormone. It has the potential to increase muscular size and strength, repair connective tissue, and decrease recovery time—all of which can enhance performance in sports.* I was not good at much, but I could shoot a three-inch group of arrows at forty yards. There was an almost meditative quality to holding in the breath while aiming, releasing the air as one releases the arrows.

23.

When the bones fuse, the spine loses its normal flexibility and becomes rigid. The rib cage also may fuse, which can limit normal chest expansion and make breathing more difficult.

24.

Once, when I shot the bright orange nock off the end of my arrow with another arrow, I showed it to my father. He held it in his hands and looked back at me in a way I kept trying, for years, to replicate. I kept that arrow in my room for the rest of high school, held horizontally between a shoulder-mounted buck's antlers.

25.

I have never seen a deer in velvet, at least not alive. But I've seen videos of bucks shaking their heads in the air at the end of September. They are trying to shake free any velvet still hanging after they've rubbed against a tree. At that point, the growing is done.

26.

I no longer hunt. And each season, my father and I have less in common.

27.

New Zealand is the world's largest producer of deer antler velvet. As of 2021, New Zealand had an estimated 841,993 farmed deer. That same year, NZ$79 million (over US$49 million) was made on farmed deer antler velvet alone. They don't kill the deer to harvest the velvet. The removal of the velvet is much gentler than I imagine. *100 tons of fresh antler . . . yields about 30 tons of dried product.*

28.

In Alabama, my parents' neighbor has a small deer farm, a different kind of deer farm, behind his house. It's high-fenced so the deer can't escape. He sells the bucks to men who pay thousands to shoot the deer in another high-fenced area. I think of those men's fathers, now long dead, and what those men are trying to prove to them.

29.

My father was at his hunting club in south Alabama when he got a call from my mother that I had been almost arrested by a cop. My friend and I had been drinking in his blue Ranger behind the Hoover Met, tossing the empty bottles into the edge of the woods where the parking lot ended. My father was pissed he had to leave the client he was entertaining to drive three hours back home. I woke up to him ripping me out of bed by the back of my t-shirt, then breaking a ruler against his desk, tears in his eyes. I thought he might kill me.

30.

Violence was a family tradition. My father, his father, his father's father. Each beating their sons, their wives, or now, the emotional abuse toward me and my sister. I think of the control that violence gave them, how they held on to it like two fistfuls of sand. I think of the violence in my own body, my body against my body, and how I wanted the violence to end.

31.

If you don't want to take the pills, the deer antler velvet can be steeped in hot water and can be drunk like a hot tea. *Warm in nature and sweet and salty in flavor,* lù róng *(velvet deerhorn) supplements kidney yáng, strengthens sinew and bone, boosts sinew and marrow, and nourishes the blood.* This tea, when bloomed in a pot, looks like brain tissue under a microscope. The tea, besides having thin slices of dried velvet, can include herbs to enhance the flavor and effects. I think of Earl Grey, of bergamot. I think of lemongrass and orange peel. I think of steam rising before disappearing.

32.

I wake up in pain. I can only take one 200 mg pill of Celebrex twice a day. NSAIDs (nonsteroidal anti-inflammatory drugs) can be brutal on the stomach, even though this pill is supposedly the gentlest of that category. Healing is not an option for me; it can't be the goal. Moving forward is.

33.

Each year my father and I grow further apart, like a scattered grouping of bullets from 300 yards away. I ask him at holidays how the hunting season's been. He tells me of the pattern of the moon, the movements of the deer, and each buck he's seen. On the couch, we sit and look at pictures from a game camera he mounted on a tree on his leased hunting property. We see a ten-point, a four-point, two racoons, and a handful of does. The bucks are still in velvet in the photos. The green glow of the night-vision camera makes them look ethereal, as if they are looking back at us, but already beyond death. Their eyes lit up, they are looking past the camera at something beyond us both.

34.

I have no choice but to shed velvet. I wish I could stop growing antlers, anything my father can count and measure year to year. But there is no shedding of my bones, no escape of the body.

35.

I remember my father taking me down a path in the woods, I was a kid, I can't remember which year this was, and he showed me the trees that the deer rubbed the velvet off on. He took my hand and let me feel where the bark was gone and the tree stood bare. The buck had scraped their rack against the tree, over and over, until the velvet finally dropped, curled like bark, and they could, at least for this season, stop growing. They could move on deeper into the woods.

WHEN MY FATHER TELLS ME I HAD A GREAT CHILDHOOD

I don't say   his temper was a sun
flare   his belt across my back
I don't say   his word ever the last

sound each afternoon through
the hallways   I don't say   muscadine
say   buckeye say   serrated say

the woods   the only place I felt safe
I don't say my shirt   ripped down the back
like a sheet of paper   don't say   I knew

one day he would kill me   or I would have to
kill him   don't say   a word as I tremble
next to my bed   I don't say   my prayers

to the god of that cold house   I don't
say   anything back   I get up off my knees

III

SONNET OF LITTLE FAITH

The rain pressing the maple leaves looks
like broken green piano keys. This view
out my bedroom window, this TV without
sound. I prayed for snow, not wet sunlight.

In a clearing, I once asked God to hold
my sadness and was told to build
a bigger heart. A bigger ark. A better window
to clean the smudges off each morning.

In the maple tree, a cardinal looks covered
in its own blood. He sees himself in the dirty glass
and tries to attack his shade. For two hours.
He dives, crashes, and repeats, steam rising

through the branches. When I go outside
to save him by scaring him, he's already gone.

ELEGY ON THE WHOLE

my grandfather   at 48 he had
a stroke   the doctors said he wouldn't
make it he   did he spent the rest

of   his life in a wheelchair   when I was
a kid   he would go with me   around
his neighborhood   and as I walked

next to him   I heard the sound
of his leather fingerless gloves   hiss
against the wheels   as he told me

about each neighbor   last night
he died   alone in his nursing home
they told me my mother   his daughter

they couldn't   find his wedding ring
it had   had it just slipped off   from all
the weight he'd lost   I in my anger my grief

I thought a nurse stole it   that was
a place to set the blame   a moment
of weakness it was   found safe

in the front office   my father says
thank God says   thank God he is
in heaven now   says he is now whole

meaning   his legs were no longer paralyzed
no longer   as the Lord in Capernaum
as the Lord said   to the man

who was paralyzed   Arise
and take up thy bed   and walk
but whole he was   he wasn't

not whole   he wasn't my father's view
of wholeness   as if ever since
the stroke   he was only   part himself

in my father's eyes   as if his body
was a prayer   that could be answered
as if the body could ever be   a measure

an accurate measure   of anything
let alone wholeness   as if   the kingdom
of my Lord   He gives us back

on the day   we ascend not
who we were on earth but   who
others   always wanted   us to be

THE MORNING AFTER THE
MOST RECENT SHOOTING I SAW

a guy on campus with a tank top that read
Keep Calm and Carry One beneath an image
of a Beretta. The news came in last night
like a slow-rolling storm: fifty dead, the shooter
surrounded by his arsenal, mowing the concert
down from a hotel window. I can picture
the gleam of late afternoon light off
the forty-three-story hotel like some silver bar
stuck in the sand. Like a bullet casing blown
against the horizon. I am not comforted
by the morning after the night. I turn off
the TV and close the blinds. After selling
my .30-06 to pay for a new computer,
I give my father the old scope, the bust
of a whitetail on the center of its knob,
the brushed metal like a stone I held in my hands.
I look through it at the kitchen table
as if standing on the bow of a boat
looking at a coastline coming into view.
Instead I see the blur of my father in front
of me. He jokingly tells me he's going to
put the scope on his assault rifle. I don't laugh.
Weeks before, he had asked me to go
to the Steel City shooting range with him. *It's fun,*
he said. *We could line some things up, we could fill
some things full of holes.* How could I talk
to him about loss? My father the gun,
my father the gunpowder that only took
one spark to set off, my father the lead—
but I know I can't. I don't get what I want.

My father tightens the scope rings
with the Leatherman he keeps on his belt,
looks down the scope to me sitting
at the kitchen table, where
from this distance, I'm upside down.

in the hallway   of my high school   my friend slipped me
a burned CD of David Allan Coe   between classes   saying
I think you'll like this   I nodded or didn't   I don't

remember   either way in the parking lot   of my high school
John raised a Confederate flag   in the bed of his Chevy
the tires edging out   of the wheel well   the truck lifted

eight inches   brush guard gleaming   like chrome prison bars
I walked to my own car   to go home   heard the throaty growl
his exhaust   clouding the air   as he drove away

just fast enough for the flag to wave   this was Pelham
this was Alabama   but even then   I could feel
a crack   forming across each hallway   across every green locker

this was years before the Nathan Bedford Forrest monument
the Confederate general   would be dethroned
covered in pink paint   his mouth agape   as if

somehow surprised   his horse on its back legs   sword
in the air   gun aimed behind him   forever pointing
to that backwards past   that would always footnote

my state in its sins   this was before *THEY WERE
RACISTS* was spray-painted in red on the Robert E. Lee
monument in Centennial Park   I didn't even shake my head

when John's truck   pulled past me   or at the jokes
he told at our lunch table   now I wish I could've gone
back to those afternoons   snuck out before the bell

doused that flag in kerosene   before lighting a match
wish I could've watched John walk up to   a bed full of ash
but I wouldn't stand up to anyone back then   too worried

about fitting in   so I nodded to John   the sort of nod
men give to say what they won't say   a nod layered
a nod as he passed   the warm exhaust almost choking me

ELEGY WITH TEETH

in high school   I never opened my mouth
but was voted somehow   best smile
my senior year   I had my mother's teeth
and my father's teeth   I saw them in the mirror
my father's mouth   a fuse   my mother's mouth

a garden   I watched his mouth   I watched
his mouth a lot   at dinner   I kept silent
as my father told me Black people   learned
to cheat the government   for handouts
his hand was   clenched around a fork

we had just prayed   over our dinner
thanked God for our blessings   my father
always ate in an angry way   as if   the meatloaf
had done something to him   he would say
a Black man didn't say   hello   back to him

at the lumberyard   the man didn't smile
the man didn't   not smile either   my father
smiled after saying *the way I see it*   before
saying he felt   discriminated against   I was
taught so much by my father   I would

later unlearn   I was taught in high school
the history of our fathers   all the forefathers
but not   their sins   I was taught
George Washington's teeth were   wood
and I imagined   the pines outside

the classroom window   but not the history
of the bodies   that hung from them
Ray Porter   August 1891   charge
not given   Two unnamed men   September
John Brown   October   charged with

testifying against whites   Sam Wright
October   Two unnamed men   February
charged with incendiarism   April
April April   April   I can imagine
my great-grandfather there   beneath

the branches   his smile lit like a torch
not even dressed in his white robes   this time
this violence was   a social occasion for him
at night before   he'd wake up and go to work
at Fannin County High School   I survived

staying silent   which I later learned was
selfish like   old George the bastard
his teeth were never   made of wood
they were made of slaves' teeth   dead or
alive still   I wasn't sure   and once in a museum

many years later   I saw those teeth next to
a tuft of hair   elements of the body
devoid of a body   the teeth set curved
in a lead jaw   with springs that helped them
open   that held the teeth   in place

against the gums   and from the other side
of the glass   the teeth looked like they were
trying to open   but were still
after hundreds of years   held shut by
those who   forced them to smile

WHEN MY ALABAMA

starts to show   when I think   almost
say   what I was taught   growing up
growing up white   in Alabama means

you grow up   believing you are better
a gravel driveway led to my house
surrounded   no   protected by the woods

we had a cast-iron gate   an entrance
laid with stone   our name engraved
as if my father meant to show our Alabama

our money like a flag   there are so many
words I said to fit in   in my Alabama
those words a noose   waiting to be tied

when my Alabama is an instrument of death
to anyone not white   when I'm taught how
to become   if I become   my father

what my father   is   his hands tying the knot
the hangman's knot   tightening the rope
my whiteness was   is an instrument

of death   when my Alabama is my Alabama
I leave the state   wanting to erase
each magnolia flower   burning atop the water

like a paper lantern that never   rose to the sky
the pond in front of my parent's house
down a foot   in the heat of the summer

when each pine gave me shade   but I knew
the cost of each branch   each pine growing
taller each year with me   until one year

I did not recognize the woods   that once
held tree forts   made from lumber my father
threw out   those places I made to make myself

feel safe   I had the privilege of privacy
but when my Alabama is   no longer
my Alabama   when I want to leave

what I've already left   I can't escape my soil
my dirt   but I can do better   I must
my Alabama can't be   entirely forsaken

not yet   my terrible beautiful love   my Alabama
I can't sing   my mouth a cannon   my mouth
a cannon stuffed full of daisies   still a cannon

still capable of violence despite the beauty
I can hear   the music my Alabama it plays to me
but there is no place on this earth I can

run from my own prejudice   I am rebuilding
the engine of my head   but no longer
from the same parts   to keep the Pelham

out of my brain   and my brain out of
my mouth   when my Alabama is an instrument
I can't forget   how to play   I know I can

only hear the music if I listen   when
I listen   I must listen to overlay the song
I was taught with the song I must pass on

each note plucked on barbed wire   is full of rust
the banjo must be restrung   and new
notes written   behind no gates   no violence

my ear against the dirt   I must listen
no matter how loud the song gets   I must
listen when my Alabama   calls me home

WHEN THE COP TELLS US

to call our parents we do: we had been caught
drinking Smirnoff Green Apple behind

the Hoover Met. Then the cop tells us
he would've taken us in, my friend and I,

if we looked more scummy. At seventeen,
I believed this to be luck, as one might

believe the rain stopping right when you walk
to your car, or a string of green lights, I believed

that where we parked my friend's truck
in the dark of that parking lot was a safe place

to drink on a Wednesday night, our two outlines
slumped against the truck bed throwing

the empty bottles into the edge of the woods.
Now, I see there is no luck in these situations:

we were white, and so was the cop
with his shining bald white head. If we'd been

Black we wouldn't have been given the chance
to call our parents, we wouldn't have been given

anything at all. And so we walked free. For almost
a decade later I believed in luck, in what

I thought we got ourselves out of, not realizing
our skin had opened an escape hatch

and would again and again and again.

ELEGY WITH A WAVELENGTH OF SOUND

That was the summer I thought I was healthy enough
to come off my meds completely, and we went

to Cascades Park together to play Pokémon GO, and you
were only in town a week, for work, and were staying

in my spare bedroom. We hadn't been outside
an hour before the rain came, so typical in summer,

turning to steam before the downpour even stopped,
the steam like some ghost being swatted away

by each droplet against it, the concrete of the sidewalk
darkening its shade of gray like a man's gray trench coat

as he pulls it tight against his body, against the cold
of a New York February, which he is used to by now,

should know better than to wear this thin coat,
more decorative than anything else, on his way

to his ex-wife's house to pick up the last
of his things that she at least took the time

and care to box up before he got there. And of course
we forgot an umbrella and so were left to run

across the park in the rain, but I swear, in those
summer months, I felt a new perception lifting

—peeking behind the holy curtain of prescription—
that I hadn't felt in years, but we were there,

in the park, and you had just caught something great,
but everything for me was humming, anxiety

like a wavelength of sound. I kept rubbing my arms
as if cold. You asked if I was alright and I said

of course, of course. We were in a patch of grass near
the water, we could've been two lone fishermen, adrift

in the escape a game allows, adrift upon some high
wave that I could see had to crash, as every time

I was happy I was just waiting for that dark surge
to pull me under again, but then I caught a Cubone,

which I had never seen before, that Pokémon who wears
his mother's skull over his head, carries a femur bone

(also hers?) around as a weapon, and I thought
I had never seen a creature so steeped

in grief—everything he looks through is through
his mother's empty eye sockets, those bone holes

like glasses with the lenses punched out, knowing
he could fill her skull with his but he could not

bring her back—that walking loss, I had never felt
so close to anything before, but he could evolve,

I could evolve him in the game to the next version
of himself, I could watch her watch him grow.

NOTES ON DEPRESSION

7:12 a.m.

The news is on. It's Saturday,
but there's still news. The screen
on mute, the car's on fire, footage
shaky: another bombing, or shooting,
or missing person. You could be
the person missing, almost. You won't
be able to watch after ten minutes.
Too much. Outside, it's bright, it's morning,
it's terrible, but inside, it's worse.

7:47 a.m.

You don't sleep. Or, if you do, never
well enough. You didn't last night,
up thinking of her again, her brown hair
falling across her blue eyes, her leaving
you because you know that's what you
deserve but you wake up
and she's still here, next to you.

7:49 a.m.

In the mirror, a man. He looks like
you, or a version of you. Reach out
your hand. Touch your face. Wipe
the sauce off your cheek from
the half-eaten burrito left out
on the coffee table from last night. Clean
yourself up. You look like a goddamn mess.

12:04 p.m.

If the medicine worked, it'd be
working. Don't forget to take it
anyway. Did you take it yet today?
You can never remember. Paxil.
Lamictal. Klonopin. Lithium, the old
staple. In your pocket everyday
you carry a pillbox you'll take into
a bathroom stall on your lunch break
during workdays. Little fire
extinguishers, you call them. You swallow
them dry, walk out the same.

3:14 p.m.

Your parents call. This time, you
pick up the phone. They tell you
at least you're not as bad
as last summer, all those hospitals.
Your father says you sound
like a zombie. You laugh to be polite.

6:32 p.m.

Finally, you go outside. Today
you're at least getting out of
the house. You've checked the mail
four times already. Besides bills,
you get letters only on your birthday.
The aluminum of the box
with your name card reminds you
of one of those morgue refrigerators.

6:36 p.m.

You stand next to an oak tree
with Spanish moss outside
your apartment building. You used to love
trees. You used to love a lot of things:
sundials, apple slices, Christmas lights
strung from porch railings, peanut butter.
Put your cigarette out on the bark, go back
inside. After all this time gone,
she'll wonder where you've been.

WHEN MY BROTHER TELLS ME
I'M OBSESSED WITH SADNESS

across the living room of the trailer
we live in   he does so   to hurt me
I can't argue exactly   when my depression
has almost killed me five   no six times

it's hard not to be obsessed with your own shadow
I don't tell him   he is right   and wrong
he is   looking up into a tree   deep
in the woods   at a bird he tries to match

with the one in the field guide   a bird
just too far away to see   the silver and rust
of its plumage   but one he cups his hands
to whistle at regardless   I don't tell him

I love him   and that's why when he calls me
by the wrong name   I will always answer

SEASIDE MEDITATION

Even the weeds that grow around
a pine tree are destined for stealing
the rainwater out of the dirt itself
like a dog lapping up communion water
in a church by the sea. Let's make it
a converted lighthouse with a pew
just wide enough for two people
not including the priest, who sits
where the light used to be, and tosses
down wafers that fall like seeds
from a pine cone, spiraling in the air.
Even a knife has aspirations, dreams
of all the cucumbers and tomatoes
it could slice. I do not want to
sharpen the blade, nor be the arm
that extends the violence. I am waiting
by the ocean for the purple flag
to be lowered, for the waves to settle
into whitecaps, I am waiting
for the undertow to pull me out
and fill my lungs. I will be buried
up to my neck, with fake sand legs
and fake sand breasts, my face
will burn in the sun if the sun
comes out today. I want the waves
to greet me, and I want no choice
but to sink beneath them. The sand
will hold me down like a mother
shielding a child in a coat closet
as a storm pelts at the windows.
I will be whole through this,
as whole as sand together can be.

ON DISHES AND MY FATHER

I always save up enough dishes to wash
when returning my father's call. I need

to keep my hands busy when the conversation
stalls and I've run out of small talk

to fill the air. My hands are full of soap
and sponge, green apple scent in the steam,

my hands turn red under the water.
My father's voice rumbles in my earbuds,

which means I hear him on both sides
of my head, inside my ears, as close to the skull

as he can get. I don't bring up my sister,
how disappointed he is in her again.

I don't bring up how labored these calls
have become, or how I don't forgive him

for the years of emotional abuse. That can
wait. Another call. Another dish. The pan

I'm scrubbing is full of the crusted smear
of melted cheese from last night. I work

at it until the next pause. When my father calls
again, I don't pick up. I wait for more dishes.

WHEN MY FRIEND TELLS ME MY FATHER DOESN'T SEEM THAT BAD

at lunch before my wedding   I agree   because of course
my father   can be a tree full of leaves   in the summer

my friend stood off near the corner   of my wedding reception
beer in hand   my father's smiling face atop his stiff body

I love my friend   who traveled three states to be there
that day   when my father would travel I would be

so excited he was leaving   still too young to know
why   I felt safe   and I love my friend but I can't

give him the memory of my father in the fire   of an afternoon full
of broken glass from the picture frame   hit against his desk

to make a point   my constant dread of when he came home
later and later   my friend is somewhat joking I know

but like a joke followed with *no offense*   there is a layer
of seriousness   my father has mellowed in his age

a dormant volcano   still smelling of sulfur   I am walking
the smooth black lava   it has cooled

to a sheen in the afternoon light   it is almost as beautiful
as a smile   but it covers   what it has burned

ADMISSION WITH A THOUSAND DEAD BIRDS

after the thunderstorm   a thousand birds fell from the sky
pulled damp to the earth   the grackles   European

starlings   red-winged blackbirds   filling trash bags
of those who picked them up in Missouri fields   and I admit

I don't know where poems come from   or how they are
given   this morning while reading   I started

an argument with my wife   over nothing
and she thunders off   leaving me   anxiety

electricity   and I admit   I caused
the storm   knowing the truth doesn't help it go down

any easier   I admit   those birds took off from their branches
expecting to land where they chose   their feathers

catching the wind in their descent   the branch
doesn't wait for us to land   or the hard ground

to take us in like a prayer   or a door closing
in a house you share

ON THE WAY TO THE READING

I walked out of my apartment building
and in the car parked nose-out next to mine
a woman's ankles were high in the air,

and at first I thought in the front seat
but a few seconds later it became clear
it was the back seat. And they moved

in that gray darkness ever so slightly
as if rocked by the ocean at night.
When I got close enough to unlock

my car door, her ankles stopped
moving, but not before I saw the tattoo
on her ankle of a daisy. I hadn't

had sex in what seemed like months,
and maybe that's normal when you've
been with someone for years, but I

couldn't help envying this couple—
to find a not-so-secluded parking lot
with a busted-out streetlamp hanging over

them like some terrible angel, to say
we will be beautiful in this back seat
even if someone catches us full of light

and glowing. The reading an hour later
almost put me to sleep, and all I could
think about the whole time were her toes

gently touching that ceiling, and how
I'd interrupted their one moment
of escape in the day, and how I hoped

they continued what they started, continued
going where they planned after I drove
away from them into the night.

no bridge on them yet   stuck holding
      nothing midair across the six-lane interstate
stoic in concrete uniformness   lag bolts
      waiting for purpose in the silvered air

I pass them by in my car   going nowhere
      important   the grocery store probably   passing
underneath the air they hold up   the light like
      the yellow line on the road   next to the rumble

strip holding small pockets of rain from last night
      the air full of possibility   knowing the future
in each thread of the column's bolts   spiraling
      upwards towards heaven like spikes at the bottom

of a pit in a dark cave passage   a trap
      built to catch angels as they fall to earth

ODE TO MY PECTUS EXCAVATUM

or my sunken chest, visible each time
I bow my head in prayer, my own body

falls in on itself, my heart a sinkhole,
a cenote. I trace my breastbone

with my fingers, feeling the air
where the ribs should be, and I recall

in the locker room, changing out
of my gym clothes, the boy who said

you could eat a bowl of cereal out of
my chest. And maybe he's right—

maybe I have made a meal of my heart
and broken body. In a video my father

sends me, my nephew climbs into
my father's bed to wake him up,

then blows on his stomach, laughing
at the noise. With his shirt up, I can see,

even through the grain of the video,
my father's own sunken chest, a valley

where no crops will grow. I spent
years inside the empty cathedral

of my father's chest, years building
each pew from a tree fallen every storm.

Years thinking if my body matched
my father's, then I must be him. That I had to

become him. I spent years unlearning this.
From the angle of the camera, there is

a shadow on his breastbone, as it
rises and falls in the morning light.

As a child, I laid my palm into
the indentation of my father's shirt.

He said our nightly prayers should be
of thanks. I cannot praise my body

while within it. I cannot remember
the trees until the trees become memory.

When I kneel, I see only the shadows
carved in my chest, so I am distracted

by my own inadequacy, the sound
of the cardinal in the front yard.

I cannot give thanks for what I'm not
thankful for. And so when I pray I pray

for a better chest, one larger, one that
can hold my father and I within it.

I pray for rainwater to gather in the gutters
of my bones, in the hollow of my center.

I pray that if I can't leave this cave
of my body—if the light from above

only plays off the water and the limestone—
I make within it a home.

NESTING

How the robin takes, places, weaves
each piece of pine needle into the nest,
forming the shape slow as snowfall. She pulls

the silverware tray from the box I packed
earlier, sets it on the table still crooked
on the hardwood. How her arms in this new

place, our first home. How I can't help
but watch the beauty of each muscle, each
finger delicate as a branch. Each time the robin

comes back to its nest, how deliberate, it knows
the pine nest it makes against any other brush.
Each return of the bird is obsessive, fixed

in the path from field to tree and back again.
I'm reorganizing the Ajax and floor polish
below the sink. I push the chairs under

the table, everything in its place. Her arms
move the air like feathers. How strange
to not want to leave, for once to not want

to flee at the first sign of danger, like the robin
before the hawk. As she takes another box
from my hands, she weaves her arms into mine.

ELEGY FOR ANOTHER
LATE-NIGHT PHONE CALL

Another drop in the bucket, how he
asked how the weather was

up here, said words.
I stopped therapy, I told him.

We never saw the same sun
the same. School days we wouldn't

talk more than a glance
when he entered the room,

eyes like a lighthouse beacon.
I was the rocks, or he was, one of us

crashing into the other. Now older,
I have to check each stove knob

three times before I can leave
my house. Father, your hands

were storms. Have I only
imagined you were ever there?

I'm trying to understand.
Father, I forgive you

or I don't. If I say I'm coming home,
please leave the porch light on.

Page 19   "People as Seasons as People" is after the Modest Mouse song "People as Places as People."

Page 45, section 4; *46*, section 8; *47*, section 11; *48*, sections 19 and 20; and *49*, section 27 of "Velvet" quote or paraphrase from Subhuti Dharmananda's article "DEER ANTLER: to Nourish Blood, Bone, and Joints," published in the *Institute for Traditional Medicine* in January 2005 (http://www.itmonline.org/arts/antler.htm).

Page 46   Section 9 of "Velvet" quotes from the webpage "What is Ankylosing spondylitis," published by the Autoimmune Association (https://autoimmune.org/disease-information/ankylosing -spondylitis/).

Page 46   Section 10 of "Velvet" quotes from the webpage "Ankylosing Spondylitis Symptoms," published by the Arthritis Foundation (www.arthritis.org/about-arthritis/types/ankylosing-spondylitis /symptoms.php).

Page 47   Section 14 of "Velvet" paraphrases from "What is Deer Antler Velvet (DAV)? Rob Riches Explains," a video on YouTube, uploaded by Antler Farms on September 26, 2017.

Page 48   Section 17 of "Velvet" quotes from the wall text for *Hunter Slaying a Stag* by Nicolas Coustou, a statue located in the Musée du Louvre in Paris.

Page 49   Section 22 of "Velvet" quotes from the webpage "Deer Antler Velvet for Bodybuilding," published by Antler Farms (https:// antlerfarms.com/blogs/articles/deer-antler-velvet-for-bodybuilding).

Page 49   Section 23 of "Velvet" quotes from the webpage "Ankylosing Spondylitis," published by the Arthritis Foundation of Asia (https:// www.arthritisfoundationasia.com/ankylosing-spondylitis.html).

Page 49   Section 27 of "Velvet": The first sentence quotes from the webpage "Deer Antler Velvet in New Zealand," published by Julius

Cermak (https://deerantlervelvet.com/deer-antler-velvet-in-new
-zealand). The second and third sentences paraphrase from the
webpage "Deer Industry Statistics," published by Statistics New
Zealand and Deer Industry New Zealand (https://www.deernz.org
/home/deer-industry-new-zealand/statistics/). This work includes
Stats NZ's data, which is licensed by Stats NZ for reuse under
the Creative Commons Attribution 4.0 International license.
According to Deer Industry New Zealand, during velvet harvesting,
the farmed deer are sedated using pole syringes, sedated by hand, or
held in a padded hydraulic cradle while local anesthetic is applied.
The last sentence quotes from the webpage "Velvet Demand,"
published by the New Zealand Ministry of Agriculture and
Forestry (http://www.maf.govt.nz/mafnet/rural-nz/profitability-and
-economics/structural-change/market-dynamics-for-venison/conf4
-04.htm) and is cited in "DEER ANTLER to Nourish Blood,
Bone, and Joints" by Subhuti Dharmananda.

Page 50   Section 31 of "Velvet" quotes from the book *Ten Lectures
*on the Use of Medicinals from the Personal Experience of Jiāo
Shù-Dé*, section 33, "Lú róng, velvet deerhorn (Cervi Cornu
Pantotrichum)," written by Jiāo Shù-Dé, translated by Craig
Mitchell, Nigel Wiseman, Marnae Ergil, and Shelly Ochs and
published by Paradigm Publications in 2003.

Pages 56–57   "Elegy on the Whole" quotes and paraphrases Mark 2:9
KJV.

Pages 62–63   The information about the lynchings in "Elegy with
Teeth" comes from the document "Lynchings in Alabama,"
complied by the Alabama Department of Archives and History on
February 18, 1921, by Monroe N. Work, the director of records
and research at the Tuskegee Institute. This document details the
lynchings in Alabama during the years 1871 to 1920.

Page 77   "Admission with a Thousand Dead Birds" references the
article "More than 1,000 birds died when a thunderstorm with
lightning and strong winds hit a Missouri town," by Christina
Zadanowicz, published by CNN on March 6, 2020.

Page 83   "Nesting" is for Molly.

THANK-YOUS

Many thanks to the following people for their help with and belief in this manuscript at every stage: Rita Mookerjee, Dustin Pearson, Tanya Grae, K. Iver, and Matt Kelsey. And for their friendship, thank you even more.

To Josh Duke, Justin Fargason, Rosalyn Stilling, Tom Tooley, Rob Stephens, and the Marotta family, thank you for your support and your friendship.

Thank you to Iraida, Angela, and Jennifer for helping me stay alive long enough to finish this book.

To Marisa Siegel, Jameka Williams, and everyone at Northwestern University Press, thank you for believing in this book the way I believe in it.

To Arielle Austin, thank you for letting me use your beautiful painting *Stirring Isolation* for the cover of my book.

To you, the reader, thank you for picking up this message in a bottle. It is a gift to have this book in your hands.

And forever, Molly.

ACKNOWLEDGMENTS

Grateful acknowledgment to the editors of the following journals and anthologies, where this work (or versions of this work) first appeared:

The Adroit Journal: "A Silverfish in the Childhood" and "River"

Appalachian Review: "Ars Poetica" and "Sonnet with Bare Branches"

Beloit Poetry Journal: "When My Friend Tells Me My Father Doesn't Seem That Bad"

Blackbird: "Elegy with Teeth" and "Ode to My Pectus Excavatum"

The Boiler: "Elegy for Another Late-Night Phone Call" and "When the Cop Tells Us"

Colorado Review: "Elegy with My Great-Grandmother's Piano"

The Columbia Review: "Letter"

The Cortland Review: "Ode to Klonopin"

decomp journal: "Alabama, 2004"

DIALOGIST: "That Summer at Seaside"

Diode: "Punch List, 1994"

The Experiment Will Not Be Bound (Unbound Edition Press): "Ankylosing Spondylitis as Conductor and Brakeman"

Great River Review: "Admission with a Thousand Dead Birds" and "Gasoline"

Harpur Palate: "The Morning After the Most Recent Shooting I Saw"

Hobart: "Tracing the Pain"

JuxtaProse Literary Magazine: "People as Seasons as People"

Lake Effect: "Ode to the Pillars of the Overpass Bridge"

LIT Magazine: "Sonnet of Little Faith"

The Maine Review: "Elegy with Steam"

Meridian: "Sonnet with Chronic Illness"

Michigan Quarterly Review: "Ark"

Midway Journal: "Seaside Meditation"

Narrative magazine: "When My Brother Tells Me I'm Obsessed with Sadness" and "When My Alabama"

Nashville Review: "Aim"

Ocean State Review: "First Plea" and "Waterline"

The Offing: "Velvet"

Ploughshares: "House Made of Guns"

Poet Lore: "Open House"

Puerto del Sol: "When My Father Tells Me to Move On Already" and "Vox"

Radar Poetry: "Elegy with a Hurricane"

Redivider: "Family Reunion" and "When My Father Tells Me I Had a Great Childhood"

The Rupture: "Elegy with a Wavelength of Sound" and "On the Way to the Reading"

Southern Humanities Review: "Arrowhead"

The Threepenny Review: "Apology"

Under a Warm Green Linden: "Nesting" and "Notes on Depression"

Valparaiso Poetry Review: "On Dishes and My Father"